Searchlight
BOOKS

How Does
Your Body
Work?

Your

Skeletal
System

Caroline Arnold

Lerner Publications Company
Minneapolis

Lerner Publications Company
A division of Lerner Publishing Group, Inc.
241 First Avenue North
Minneapolis, MN 55401 U.S.A.

Website address: www.lernerbooks.com

Library of Congress Cataloging-in-Publication Data

Arnold, Caroline.
    Your skeletal system / by Caroline Arnold.
        p.   cm. — (Searchlight books™—How does your body work?)
    Includes index.
    ISBN 978–0–7613–7452–7 (lib. bdg. : alk. paper)
    1. Skeleton—Juvenile literature. I. Title.
    QM101.A76 2013
    611'.71—dc23   2011044175

Manufactured in the United States of America
1 – CG – 7/15/12

Contents

Chapter 1

THE BODY'S SUPPORT

Bones make up the body's skeletal system. You cannot see your bones. But you can feel them under your skin. Bones support and protect your body the way an umbrella's ribs support it.

You have bones in all parts of your body. What do bones do?

Bones are hard and strong. Most other parts of the body are soft. Bones hold up your body and give it structure.

IF YOU HAD NO BONES, YOU COULD NOT RUN, JUMP, OR DO CARTWHEELS.

Bones and Muscles

Bones and muscles work together. Muscles pull bones to make them move. Muscles attached to your arm and leg bones help you run or throw a ball. Muscles attached to your finger bones help you write or pick up a spoon.

Some bones protect organs inside your body. Your skull protects your brain. Your ribs form a cage around your heart and lungs. Your hip bones protect organs in the lower part of your body.

The muscles and bones of your hand work together to help you draw.

Chapter 2

ALL ABOUT BONES

Bones come in many sizes. Your smallest bone is in your ear. This bone is only about as big as a sesame seed. Your longest bone is in your upper leg. This bone is about one-fourth of your total height.

Your bones help you stand up straight and tall. Where is your longest bone?

Many Shapes

Bones come in many shapes. Long bones are found in your arms and legs. Long bones usually have knobby ends and a straight central shaft. Short bones are found in your wrists and ankles. Your ribs, shoulder bones, breastbone, and the bones of your skull are flat bones. The bones in your spine and inner ear have odd, bumpy shapes.

The bones in your arms and legs are long bones. Bones in other parts of your body have many different shapes.

BONE SHAPES

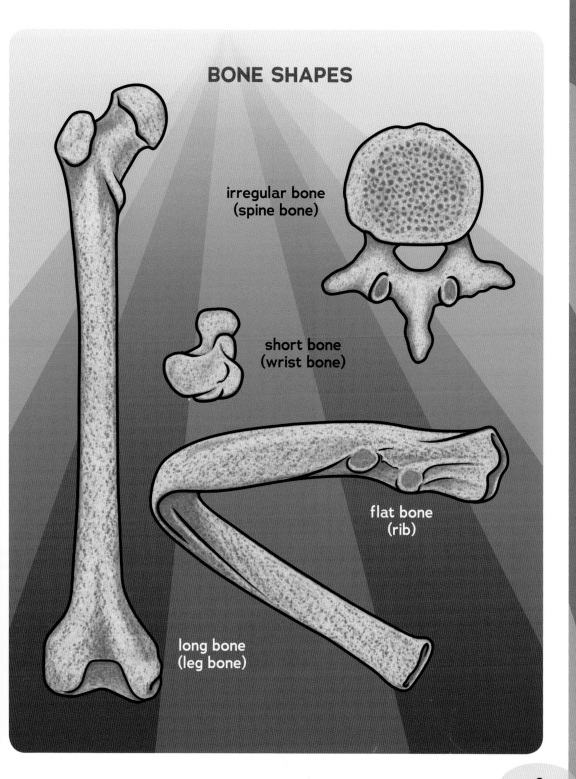

irregular bone
(spine bone)

short bone
(wrist bone)

flat bone
(rib)

long bone
(leg bone)

In and around Bones

Most of a bone's surface is covered with a thin layer of blood vessels and nerves. This layer is called the periosteum. It helps the bone grow and repair itself.

Bones are strong, but sometimes they break. This is an X-ray of a broken bone.

Beneath the periosteum is hard bone. Tiny holes in hard bone let blood vessels and nerves pass through. Under the hard bone is a layer of lighter, spongy bone. It looks something like a honeycomb.

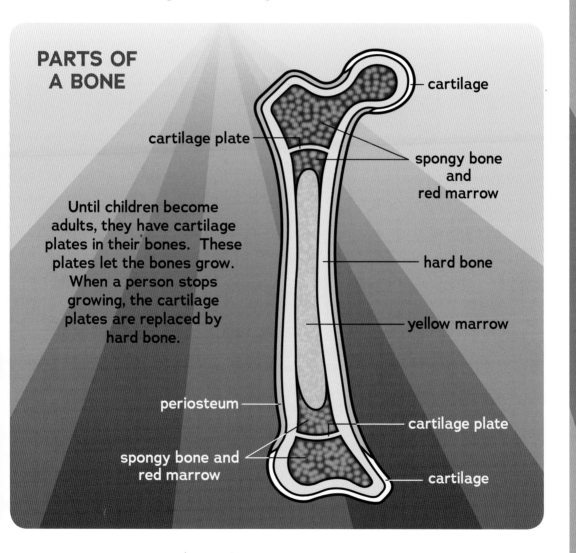

PARTS OF A BONE

cartilage plate

spongy bone and red marrow

cartilage

Until children become adults, they have cartilage plates in their bones. These plates let the bones grow. When a person stops growing, the cartilage plates are replaced by hard bone.

hard bone

yellow marrow

periosteum

cartilage plate

spongy bone and red marrow

cartilage

Bone Marrow

Most bones have a soft jellylike material in the center. This material is called marrow. Yellow bone marrow stores fat. Red bone marrow makes blood cells. Your bones make thousands of new blood cells every day.

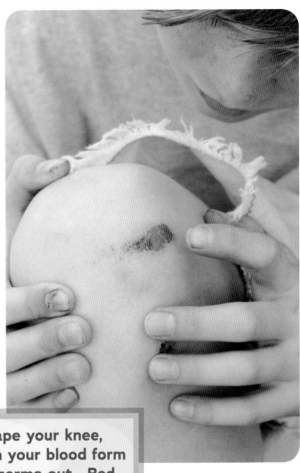

When you scrape your knee, sticky platelets in your blood form a scab to keep germs out. Red bone marrow makes platelets.

Cartilage

The ends of most bones are covered with a white material called cartilage. Cartilage protects bones where they rub against each other. You also have cartilage in your nose and ears. Cartilage is tough and slippery and can bend a little. It is not as hard as bone, but it is strong. The bones of a baby's skeleton begin as cartilage. The cartilage is slowly replaced by hard bone as the child grows.

A newborn baby's body has about 300 bones. Some of them join together as the baby grows. An adult has about 206 bones.

Chapter 3

YOUR SKELETON

Your skeleton is the framework for your body. You could not stand up or move if you did not have a skeleton. The skull is at the top of the skeleton. If you touch your head, your skull feels like one big smooth bone under the skin. But it is actually twenty-nine bones joined together. Your skull acts like a built-in helmet. It protects the organs of your head.

The bones of your head are called your skull. How many bones make up your skull?

The top of the skull covers the brain. The bones at the front of the skull support the face. Put your hands on your face. Can you feel the holes in your skull around your eyes? Your skull also has a hole for your nose and two openings for your ears.

The front of your skull
has fourteen bones
that support your face.

Each of your ears has three tiny bones inside. Sounds make these bones move. Nerves carry this information from your ear to your brain. Then you hear the sound.

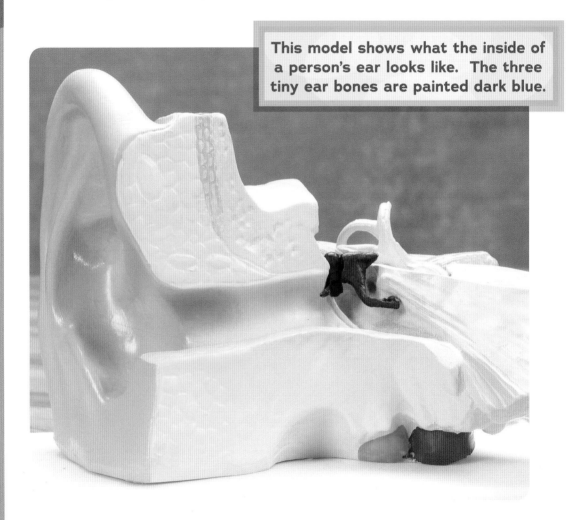

This model shows what the inside of a person's ear looks like. The three tiny ear bones are painted dark blue.

Moving Parts

The only part of the skull that can move is the lower jawbone. It moves up, down, and sideways. It helps you talk, bite, and chew.

Your teeth are attached to the bones of your jaw. Teeth are even harder than bones. Teeth are covered with a thick layer of a tough material called enamel. It protects your teeth from wearing down as you chew.

Your lower jaw helps you bite into an apple.

The Spine

Your spine connects your skull to the rest of your body. The spine is a row of thirty-three bones. Each one is called a vertebra. Together, they form a bony rod that supports your back.

A single bone cannot bend. But the spine is like a row of beads on a wire. The row bends and twists as you move. A pad of cartilage cushions each vertebra.

Your back is made of hard bones. But the bones can move to let you bend over and touch your toes.

The large, round part of each vertebra supports the body's weight. A hole through the center lets the spinal cord pass through. The spinal cord carries messages between the brain and other parts of the body. Muscles attach to bony spikes at the side and back of each vertebra. You can feel the knobs if you run your hand along your spine.

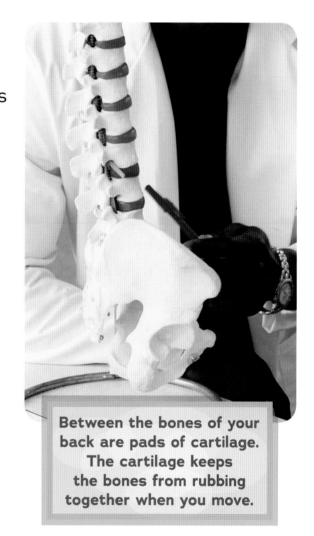

Between the bones of your back are pads of cartilage. The cartilage keeps the bones from rubbing together when you move.

Ribs and Rib Cage

The ribs are long, flat bones curving around the chest. You have twelve sets of ribs. In the back, one end of each rib is attached to the spine. In the front of the body, all the ribs except the bottom two pairs are attached to the breastbone. The bottom two pairs are called floating ribs.

Your ribs are just under the skin of your chest.

The ribs, spine, and breastbone make up the rib cage. It is like a fence around the upper body. The rib cage protects the heart, the lungs, the kidneys, the liver, and other organs.

Your rib cage also helps you breathe. When muscles lift up your rib cage, air flows into your lungs. When the muscles relax, air goes out.

The ribs protect the organs of the upper body.

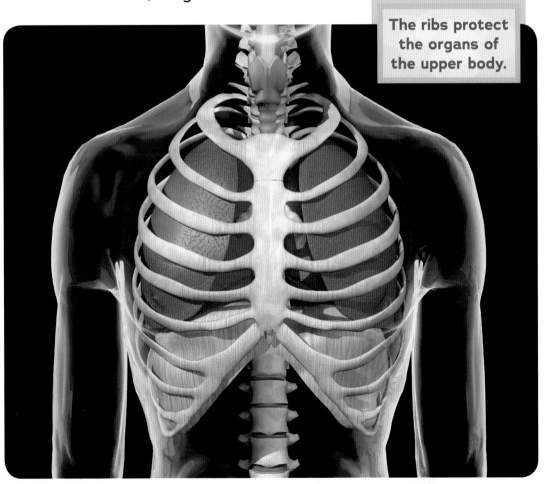

Arm and Hand Bones

Your arm bones are joined to the rest of your body at your shoulder. The shoulder bone is a strong, large, flat bone in your back. In the front, the shoulder is supported by the collarbone.

Your upper arm has one long bone. Your lower arm has two bones. Hold your lower left arm with your right hand, and then turn your left wrist. Can you feel the bones twist? These bones move so you can carry things or throw a ball.

Your arm bones can twist to help you swing a bat.

Your wrist is a group of small, knobby bones. These bones are connected to the five bones of your palm. Each of the palm bones is connected to the long bones of the fingers and thumb. You need your fingers and thumb to hold onto things.

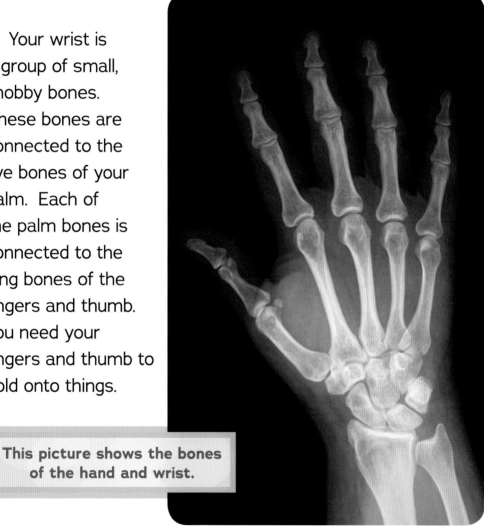

This picture shows the bones of the hand and wrist.

Hip and Leg Bones

The legs are connected to the rest of the body at the hips. The hip bones support the lower body and protect its organs. You can feel the top of your hip bones if you put your hand on your side just below your waist.

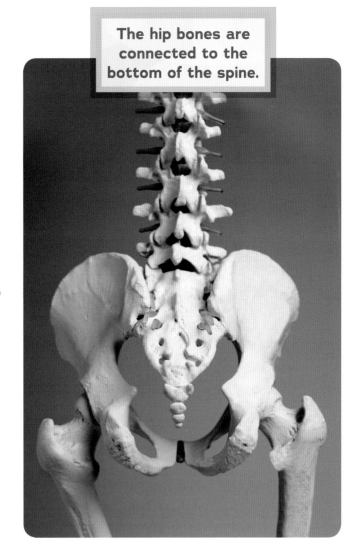

The hip bones are connected to the bottom of the spine.

The upper leg has one large bone. The lower leg has two bones that can twist just like the bones of the lower arm. These bones let the lower leg turn.

You can sit cross-legged because two bones in each leg can twist.

Have you ever fallen and bumped your knee? Your knee is covered by a small bone called the kneecap. It helps protect your knee.

WHEN YOU KNEEL, YOUR KNEES REST ON THE GROUND. YOUR KNEECAPS PROTECT THE ENDS OF YOUR LEG BONES.

Foot Bones

The bones of your feet are similar to the bones of your hands. But the foot bones cannot move as well. They are used mainly for standing, walking, and running.

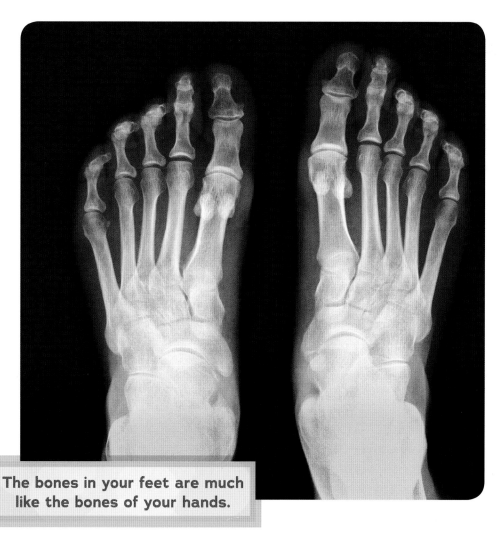

The bones in your feet are much like the bones of your hands.

Chapter 4

CONNECTING THE BONES

The place where two bones meet is called a joint. Different parts of the body have different kinds of joints.

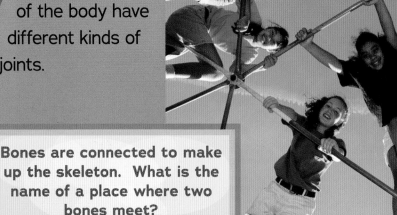

Bones are connected to make up the skeleton. What is the name of a place where two bones meet?

KINDS OF MOVING JOINTS

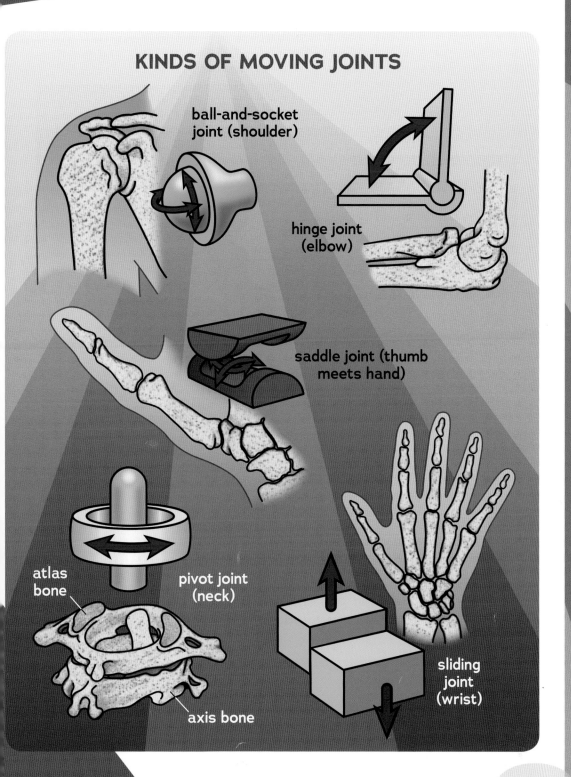

ball-and-socket joint (shoulder)

hinge joint (elbow)

saddle joint (thumb meets hand)

atlas bone

pivot joint (neck)

axis bone

sliding joint (wrist)

Moving Joints

Your shoulders and hips have ball-and-socket joints. The end of your arm or leg bone is round, like a ball. It fits into a cuplike shape in the shoulder bone or hip bone. Ball-and-socket joints let the arms and legs move in almost every direction.

The ball-and-socket joint in your shoulder lets you raise your hand above your head.

The joints of your fingers bend in only one direction. These joints are called hinge joints. They work like the hinges on a door. You also have hinge joints in your knees and elbows.

The joint of the thumb is called a saddle joint. It is shaped like a riding saddle. This joint lets you move your thumb up and down and sideways. You also have saddle joints in your wrists and ankles.

The hinge joint in your elbow bends in only one direction.

You have a special pivot joint at the top of your spine. This joint is like a ring sitting on a peg. It lets your head move from side to side and nod up and down.

The bones of your spine are connected with gliding joints. These joints let the bones slide slightly when you bend your back. But they keep the spine stiff enough to hold up your body. You also have gliding joints in your wrists and ankles.

The pivot joint in your neck lets your head turn in many different directions.

Inside the joints that move is a liquid that helps the bones to slide easily against each other. This liquid works in the same way that oil helps a machine run smoothly.

Suture Joints

Some joints fasten bones together so they do not move at all. These joints are called suture joints. Your skull is held together by suture joints. They look like zigzag lines across the bone.

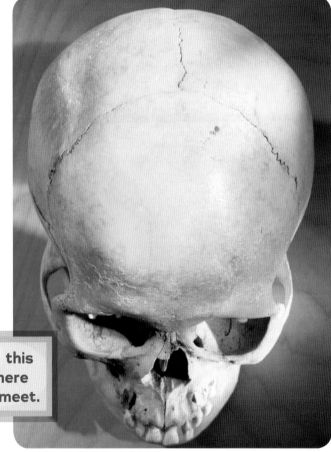

The zigzag lines on this skull are places where the different bones meet.

Ligaments and Tendons

Bones are connected with tough bands called ligaments. Ligaments wrap around the joints and hold them together. Ligaments stretch when the bones move.

MUSCLES AND BONES WORK TOGETHER.

Muscles are attached to bones by narrow bands called tendons. They are like strong strings at the ends of the muscles. Tendons let the muscles pull the bones and make them move. You can see the tendons in the back of your hand move when you bend your fingers.

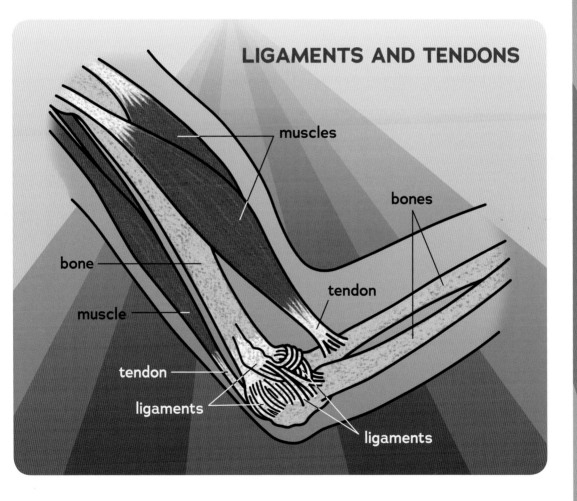

LIGAMENTS AND TENDONS

muscles

bones

bone

muscle

tendon

tendon

ligaments

ligaments

Healthy Bones

Healthy bones are part of a healthy body. You can help keep your bones strong and healthy by eating good foods and getting enough exercise. Exercise helps your bones by keeping your muscles strong. It also keeps your joints moving well.

Your skeleton is an important part of a healthy body. You couldn't stand, walk, run, or eat without it.

Drinking milk helps to make your bones strong. What other things can you do to help your bones?

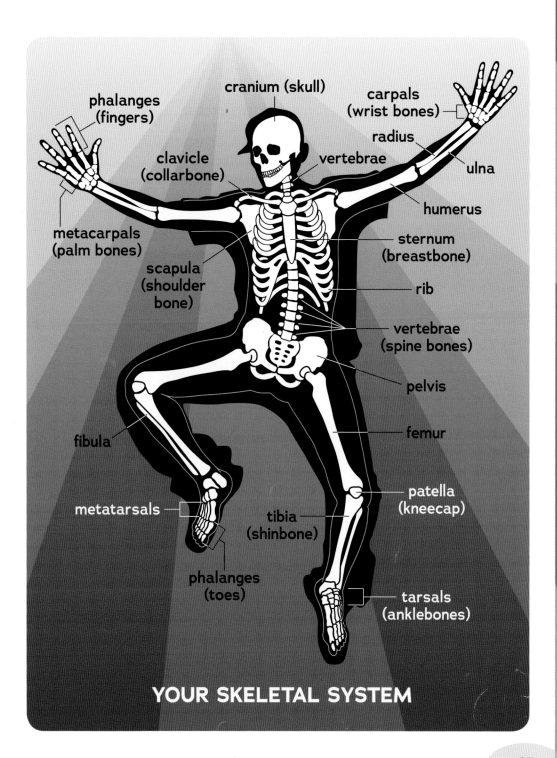

phalanges
(fingers)

cranium (skull)

carpals
(wrist bones)

radius

clavicle
(collarbone)

vertebrae

ulna

humerus

metacarpals
(palm bones)

sternum
(breastbone)

scapula
(shoulder
bone)

rib

vertebrae
(spine bones)

pelvis

fibula

femur

metatarsals

patella
(kneecap)

tibia
(shinbone)

phalanges
(toes)

tarsals
(anklebones)

YOUR SKELETAL SYSTEM

Glossary

blood vessel: a tube in the body through which blood flows

cartilage: a tough, white material that protects bones where they rub against each other

enamel: the tough material on the outside of teeth. Enamel protects your teeth from wearing down as you chew.

joint: a place where two bones meet

ligament: a strong, tough band that connects bones

marrow: a soft, jellylike material found in the center of most bones. Yellow bone marrow stores fat. Red bone marrow makes blood cells.

nerve: a fiber that carries messages between the brain and the rest of the body

organ: a part of the body that has a special purpose. The heart, lungs, and eyes are organs.

periosteum: a thin layer of blood vessels and nerves that covers most of the surface of a bone. The periosteum helps the bone grow and repair itself.

skeleton: the framework of bones in the body

skull: the bony case that protects the brain and other organs of the head

spinal cord: the thick cord that is found inside the spine. The spinal cord is made up of many nerves.

spine: the row of bones that runs down the center of the back. The spine is also called the backbone.

tendon: a tough band that connects muscles to bones

vertebra: one of the thirty-three bones of the spine

Learn More about the Skeletal System

Books

Burstein, John. *The Mighty Muscular-Skeletal System*. New York: Crabtree, 2009. Burstein takes a lively look at muscles and bones.

Cobb, Vicki. *Your Body Battles a Broken Bone*. Minneapolis: Millbrook Press, 2009. Popular science writer Cobb explains how the human body heals a broken bone.

Johnson, Rebecca L. *Your Muscular System*. Minneapolis: Lerner Publishing Company, 2013. Learn how closely the muscular system works with the skeletal system.

Petrie, Kristin. *The Skeletal System*. Edina, MN: Abdo, 2007. Investigate the skeletal system in this interesting read.

Websites

Enchanted Learning: Human Skeleton
http://www.enchantedlearning.com/subjects/anatomy/skeleton
This website provides basic information about the human skeleton and features diagrams of a human skeleton and of the spine and skull.

IMCPL Kids' Info Guide: Skeletal System
http://www.imcpl.org/kids/guides/health/skeletalsystem.html
This page from the Indianapolis Marion County Public Library has a list of resources you can use to learn more about the skeletal system.

KidsHealth: Your Bones
http://kidshealth.org/kid/htbw/bones.html
This article offers a detailed explanation of the skeletal system. It also includes a diagram of a bone.

Index

Photo Acknowledgments

The images in this book are used with the permission of: © Photodisc/Getty Images, pp. 4, 18, 20, 24, 26, 28, 31, 33; © PT Images/Getty Images, p. 5; © EyeWire/Getty Images, pp. 6, 8; © Todd Strand/Independent Picture Service, pp. 7, 16; © Laura Westlund/Independent Picture Service, pp. 9, 11, 29, 35, 37; © Royalty-Free/CORBIS, pp. 10, 13, 14, 19, 22, 30, 32, 36; © Suzanne Tucker/Dreamstime.com, p. 12; © Belinda Images/SuperStock, p. 15; © Anke Van Wyk/Dreamstime.com, p. 17; © 3DClinic/Getty Images, p. 21; © Shannon Tidwell/Dreamstime.com, p. 23; © iStockphoto.com/Kai Chiang, p. 25; © Itsmejust/Dreamstime.com, p. 27; © Peter Cade/Iconica/Getty Images, p. 34.

Front cover: © Sebastian Kaulitzki/Dreamstime.com.

Main body text set in Adrianna Regular 14/20.
Typeface provided by Chank.